salmonpoetry

Publishing Irish & International

Poetry Since 1981

the arts council
an chomhairle ealaíon

funding
literature
artscouncil.ie

Rogue States

Fred Johnston

Published in 2018 by
Salmon Poetry
Cliffs of Moher, County Clare, Ireland
Website: www.salmonpoetry.com
Email: info@salmonpoetry.com

ISBN 978-1-912561-25-4

Cover Artwork: © *Vladislav Krylov | Dreamstime.com*
Cover Design & Typesetting: *Siobhán Hutson*

Printed in Ireland by Sprint Print

Salmon Poetry gratefully acknowledges the support of
The Arts Council / An Chomhairle Ealaíon

for Mary Ellen

for Gerry McDonnell

for John Hogan

"Il suffisait d'être logique."

JEAN-PIERRE ABRAHAM: *Fort-Cigogne*

Acknowledgements

Acknowledgements and thanks are due to the following publications where some of these poems first appeared:

STAND, The New Statesman, Cyphers, The Interpreter's House, Orbis, The Coffee House – A Meeting-place for The Arts, The Stony Thursday Book, The Frogmore Papers, Crocott's Mail (South Africa,) *The Galway Review, The Spectator, Poetry Ireland Review, PLANET – The Welsh Internationalist, The Irish Times, Temenos Academy Review, Clare FM, Sunday Miscellany* (RTE Radio 1).

My apologies to anyone I have omitted.

A special thanks to Tom Gatti and Hugo Williams.

Contents

Cancer Unit

Oddly like a waiting-room at a train station
The same gruff fidgety anticipation
Yet an absence of baggage, an absence of destination.

Comical, almost, the way we middle-aged men
Take in the TV news, slaughters local or alien
Remote as cartoons, remote as going home again.

Absurdly thrilling, the opening of that door
The no-nonsense nurse, a glimpse of the corridor
Her files resemble old mail, one falls to the floor

A child's excitement, this human error
But no one, not one man, moves to help her
Pick up this sheaf of hope and, God knows, terror

Names are sweetly called, but not you, not yet
You're still a blank page and maybe they'll forget
Or lose you, better still; still, the train-clack fret
Not yet, not yet, not yet.

Procedure

It will be like this, a fusion in bright light of flesh and steel
Blue smocks that never tie up properly, one's backside hanging
Out like a prank; the quick jabbing nicks and scrapes, days in limbo —

Hung up between knowing and not, it's no place to be
Try reading a book while they pass sentence somewhere
And then go for tea; try to imagine love in such a storm

Better to know, pedestrian opinions say; but it isn't —
You've seen your father strain between morphine sleep
And bone-scouring fire, it comes to you in technicolor, frame

By frame. Better, you say, to hop a 'plane, outrun the thing
Commit unfathomable sin, kill an old enemy. Go beyond ordinary
Law, go down in flames. But you'll do the everyday and pay

A bill here and there, sooner or later pretend nothing happened;
Keep up the scribble, keep shtum, wash the windows —
They may stamp your visa in the end, may yet wave you through.

Surgical Strike

They think they'll find a Tora Bora they can drone over
and it won't be painless, that rooting out; later, they'll study
the images, conclude there's a safe house they've not
even considered; over the border, snug in the bone.

They'll watch for comings and goings, probe and scan, then
huddle, weigh options, someone in a trim suit scrutinising data.
A computer will whistle in a secret room, a girl with decent
legs will type up the mission, send it to me, contrive consent –

I'll bleed less by then, be ready for them: be *Good to go* –
But this is to place some abstract context over what it is,
a language construct as cold as code. I'm waiting for
a laser-guided strike, buying time, living the hit-and-miss.

Diagnosis

Now that the numbers add up
the screens have advertised their verdict
there's a yellow corridor to walk down
into the half-light of how things are changed

yet out among the parking spaces
men like you smoke illicit fags
as if nothing's happened but everything will,
precarious on the edge of no going back

the future is in a brown envelope
in the language of things dispensed, calculated
they never say much, the wise ones,
mortality is a flag snapping on a far hill –

you went in as one man and emerge
as another, knowing secret things of blood
and tissue and deep scans. You could live
well without such knowledge, or unknow it.

Hideous Fish

'Radio waves cause these aligned atoms to produce very faint signals,
– used to create cross-sectional images – like slices in a loaf of bread.'

– *from notes on MRI scans*, The Mayo Clinic

It must have been something like this
in a kamikazi one-man sub

it must have taken your breath away
the noise itself, the impulse to get out –

all very human to count down the minutes
squirm in the tubular loneliness

all the time something magnetically wretched
scans you, homing in on the hot spot

impersonal as a civil servant
takes notes on distance, diameter

that slow-set warhead on the rib
the timer set for God knows when –

who'd slide in here of his own free will
bone-dry yet drowning by other means?

Over the headphones, parched music
you've chosen yourself

to take your mind off the bang and thump
like hideous fish trying to get in

maybe they'll breach the sterile hull
nibble at you from the inside out.

Grace

'But when he saw that even this was impossible
he felt offended, lost all interest in the matter ... '

TOLSTOI, *Resurrection*

There's a TV in a high corner no one watches
the news we want isn't likely to come up there
at the Reception window there's a girl with nunish hair
but not a sound in this room, not a trickle of fresh air

Vague trundlings and metal snicks in snatches
down the corridor of a dozen soft-spoken rooms
we twist our fingers, shift our feet, no one assumes
change is good, a hothouse of panic, needling dooms

Brochures, leaflets, nurses, files in brown batches
someone's laughing in the infinite, irrelevant elsewhere
soon enough, a verdict like sacred writ, slow so you can hear
every word, numeral, percentage: murky odds made oddly clear

Stand, and in a drunk politeness hear the latches
lift on this immaculate consulting space
all white and nicely warmed; the smile on his face
a handshake, as if his diagnosis were a kind of grace.

Rogue States

i.m. Peter Kay, poet

Now we're the waiting-room brigade
daubed with crosses of invisible paint
on the forehead, scribed into ledgers
      posed in plastic chairs like art-pieces
      still lifes, or, as the French say, *natures mortes*

Not so much dead perhaps as transmuted
into the out-of-date, like the curl-cornered
magazines, we've been handled too often
      scanned but not read
      idle curiosity is for other people not

Splitting apart from the inside out, dividing
themselves, annexing bits like rogue states
not quite failed but a tad ungovernable
      stepping over a line, shape-changing
      redrawing the borders we knew by heart.

Bone Scanning

Perhaps like Superman I will see through walls
now that I've tanked up on isotopes
lighting bruise-blue veins and sparking neon
from suspect bones

the camera, smoochy as a lover
will map out the secret places where
little bumpy evils lurk
jigsawing until I am like a find in a dig

and there it is, the whole of me in middle-age
nothing for a lover to caress
a Hallowe'en thing with the ugly quiet
of the dead. Give this clatter

of razor-white calcium a name
even as its anonymity claims its non-identity
a figure polished up from a mass grave
a chip in the skull where the bullet went in

not a movement or the image will blur
as if a spirit wrestled its way out of the frame
call it a soul, if you will, it won't matter
I am my own atrocity, I know that now.

Reduction

'*Quand un homme meurt*
il doit rendre son alphabet . . . .'
BERNARD NOËL, *Portrait*

See now how the sea is not blue
low sky never an exact shade of grey
these misconceptions have always
been with me as I was taught them –

the colour of my file is red
it holds the geographies of my death
not tomorrow, perhaps, but a soon day
maps of bone, a border not what it was

here is the site of ambush, a dark spit
knifing spinesharp through reefs of rib
it puzzles them, the cosmonauts, circling
the diminishing globe of what I am, or was

they're eager for more images
they lust for certainty, but for whose sake?
I would rather not know what's
there, nor learn of its savage inhabitants –

Taught that the sea was blue
and bad weather ran to patchy grey
this black-and-white intrusiveness
shakes me, that I am reduced to this.

Bunker

'Quas extra se videre putant imagines,
   intra oculos habent.'

ROBERT BURTON, *The Anatomy of Melancholy*
(quoting Galen)

Down in Radiotherapy
This blue bunker of last resort
There's chilled laughter
Like a joke blown over ice
The magazines are out of date
The gossip at the water cooler
Is clipped like code
Not just anyone enters here –

But here is different
Hic sunt dracones
Scaly-backed nightmares
The wounded on trolleys
Knights errant and the green grail
Lights slashing the prone body in four
Holy pieces, cruciform, hapless Christs
On a gurney; that's why we whisper

Not to rouse cell-deep evils
Incarnate under our splitting bones
A cage of calcium struts and sinewy beams
A bomb going off in slow-motion –
The architect got it wrong, left
A space for this contended zone
Prone to a sly inside job, self-treason.

Vigil

'Notre porte reste ouverte même la nuit,
Chacun est libre d'y entre.'

CLARA DUPONT-MONOD, *La Passion selon Juette*

He lay on his side in a room where the door stayed open
Not a good sign in a hospital ward
A sort of dry contempt for someone so agile
So quick on his feet and with his tongue
The great silence, solid as brick, framed in that open door

I ought to have visited more often — isn't that what we say?
A tendril of remorse tickles the heart
What good does it do either of us, the still-standing,
And the shrink-wrapped form that couldn't care less
Lungs stuffed like cabbage leaves, you might say that.

We're going nowhere, not now. We're entangled here
Among the hissy tubes, the bips, the lime-green lights:
Is this what's left for language?
In my room I have his books, unreturned
Refugees, he was their country, lock and key.

New Order

I enter a new order of things
learn the language of blood tests, platelets,
reticulocytes, an *Absolute Neutrophil Count*,
lymphocetes; even the chance, however remote,
of Rocky Mountain spotted fever –
somehow I am in that zone where blood will out
where all things are fatal until proven innocent.

How did I stumble here, when did the colossus
yield to sand, where was I when the Sphinx
moved a blasted paw under my feet
and I went face-down into a deceit of years?

When did the heart fail the rose, I didn't see that
coming; with my skull in the MRI scan's pulsing
sheath, what verses did I compose to its beat?
It's a shock, I tell you, to become like everyone else
to be human, frail as God, ordinary as grass
collapsing inward, drying up, unheroic, alarmed.

Condolences

We were in a desert when we heard the news
perhaps near Aïn Sefra, it's hard now to recall
a flat plain of yellowed hallucination, a road
of black illusion on a shivering parchment,
we slopped back bottled water, dry as tombs –

here, then, a hotel room breathless as drowning
sleepless to the sound of a prayer-call;
how distance and, let's face it, time separated
us from the source of untidy grief
already sifted by the time we learned of it

sand-blasted down to its bare bones, it arrived
dulled of its sharper edge, a sketched abstraction
loose-formed as dust, almost nothing. In pencil
on a hotel postcard some sort of suitable remark
meaningless, necessary, inscrutable as a hieroglyph.

Algiers

What I can remember are taxis and a long walk by the docks
smell of oil and tar and fish-stalls by the mosque –
where were you, daughter, who crept out in photographs?

Those white buildings, white as blind eyes, and the casbah
with its deceit of lanes and entrances, and a donkey
for no reason still as held breath in the middle of the street

Where were you in all of this, can you remember for me?
I needed cheap wine and pills to keep me bouyant
someone to read the street-maps, take care of us both

Invisible to myself, was I invisible to you? Dust and blue sea,
afternoons heavy and viscous as poured concrete –
rank wine in the teeth and a tongue burnt by black tobacco

Postcards that told lies, I wrote them in the old French rooms
needing witnesses, the post-box became a confessional –
we're as out of touch now as then, images with their colours bled

Out, we may as well not have existed. Algiers did that
and the other places, exotic or plain,
I doubt we trailed a decent shadow through all that light.

Arrest

The sun always grabs us by surprise
it's yolky wash on a pub wall
the clumsy spill round the black legs of café tables.

it rains so frequently it's like the sea
trying to climb out of its skin. The beach
is a runnelled grey, an old man's face in cardiac arrest.

we have stopped being pretty, all of us
too many pills and pill-packs embarrass our pockets;
the future served up three times daily after meals.

Cloud Cover

Are you aware of me,
swaddled in this temperate tube?

the clouds are like poured
concrete, hard enough to walk on

now and then a fissure opens
on a grid of small towns, a floor

of indifferent fields, a ruck
of hills. I might tumble through

like a shot bird, and I think of it,
my clawing at the blue air, kicking

for a hold on a wall of falling;
my breath quickens, I drink

from a plastic cup a bitter hack
of in-flight wine. This is my terror,

that you will look up and see
a miles-high convulsion and spin

that you reach out forever and fail
to catch me, to break my fall.

Bet On It

Winter's a slow-dripping tap
rows of houses headstones in rain
no poetry here, just plainspeaking,
all walking-stick and flat cap

bookies office and corner shop
map out the unheroic boxing-ring
of the everyday, nothing to sing
about, life with a full-stop

yet you can bet some fool's turning
cantatas in his head,
lyricising the unliveable in the deadcalm
kitchen, while a used tea-bag's drying

on a two-ring electric heater,
cauterising the runny sore of it all
rejection notes thick as carpet in the hall
left to be tramped on, beneath the whispery meter

you can bet on it, the heart's still there
under the floorboards, hearable
only to him, unbearable
but with a rhythm, putting words in his ear.

Ascent

No doubt some will get up there before us
they're playing a different game

we came here first with ropes and failure
no one fails now, the route's well struck

you can see it all from the air, a clean perspective
postcard-clear. We came up half-blind

ice on the tongue, we couldn't make a myth
of any of it, it was hard, it hurt

the view from the top made us weep —
they are clever now, as we never were

they've made some slick evolutionary leap
become birds, become seraphim, they

grab the air in their teeth, bite down hard
chew their way up and up, swallow us whole.

Soft Spot

'Next to music, beer was best.'

CARSON McCULLERS,, *The Heart is a Lonely Hunter*

Every Sunday afternoon
mostly between four o'clock and five
I'd take the stage between rock bands
and do an acoustic set

then the front tables were
occupied by black-jacket bikers
they sent up drinks
and had a real soft spot for James Taylor

I must have been good enough
they were always there
along with the gifts of beer
and clap-and-whistle enthusiasm

but they stopped coming
when one of them died under a truck
I played on, but my audience
dwindled, the heart had gone –

or some part of the heart
that managed the flow and pulse
of what I did
you could feel the loss of that extra beat.

Watering

Why do you keep doing it —
all day in a garden not ten feet wide
digging this and planting that
watering and watering?

are you trowelling for treasure
or truffles? Human baby bones?
Some primordial hideousness —
A way under the wire, a way out?

Trying to grow a new thing,
some splendourous dazzle of a rose
or plant yourself, for that matter
grow rooted, sturdier, grow upwards

like a tree, skin-barked,
eyes for leaves, that sort of thing?
Your roots would undermine
the house, have you thought of that?

You'd be naked in winter
embarrassed in the rain. Stop, now.
Bent over, you're merely vulnerable,
and I feel like a predator

watching you from here, hearing
the chewing of the trowel skin-
ing laughable gravel. You
won't find what you're digging for

no history there and little promise —
it's been like that for years, maybe
that's all there is, what you're doing
scrabble-and-dig, watering and watering.

.

Working From A Still Point

My father never took me fishing
we had neither lakes nor rivers close at hand
we were miles from fishable waters

He recited his memories of bombs and shipwrecks
of 'planes pursuing one another in a grey sky
and of his first sighting of an iceberg

Perhaps this was fishing of another sort
somewhere in all of it was a dull regret
that things hadn't taken a different turn –

He'd toss out this line of himself
and see what it hooked, in amongst the reedy
inconsistencies there was a still point

Where he could have beached himself
happily, breathed more slowly, lived well
enough in another air, nothing unfathomable

He was happiest in the daily shallows
in filtered brightness, where light broke
in rippled intensities and the surface was near

Mundane suited him, with a pinch of risk
a football terrace on a Saturday, a bet
on a horse; poor man's shrapnel, harmless

He believed I could not see this entangled man
that it was unheroic to conjure up the torn flesh
reveal where the barbs went in and how deep.

Sand

A desert is a place without expectation.
            NADINE GORDIMER, *Telling Times*

Do you remember, as I do
the sky gone dark and the wind storming up
that grasping sand, argumentative at the doors
hissing at the windows
the sweaty fright of it, like smothering?

Surfacing, the flat huddled houses
breathed hot blue air
and all was well again. That night
sipping sour wine, we heard the camels
lament, scenting the slaughterhouse

And learned how they dripped
fat tears. How much we learned, how often
small shocks of new things
thieved our sleep, sand erasing the roads
in drifts high as hills, our love like grit

Clogging the heart. Do you remember?

Sandwork

Old sand the colour of papyrus
a dirty lemony skin of parched blown roughness
as a sick man might wear in spite of the sun –
in these lithe dunes, a scrabble of touch
and breath, eyelids shut, eyes skittish under them
a blow of grit-nip breeze in the skinny grass
scent of ammonia, the tongue-taste of salt
that silence after, like a hole in all sound,
a conductor's baton frozen in musical air –
all the walk back over the bridge
there is nothing to say, Dublin Bay ticks like a clock –
soon it will be dark all round, yet
I'll know you by your shadow's weight, a pillow's-worth of sand.

Fly

He saw her step out of the bathroom
new-showered, hair shredding down her face —
he saw her growing old under the skin of the towel
folding on her thready thighs

How had she begun, this leaf-fall woman
where had she come from in spite of him:
he could not say what needed to be said,
the spell for resurrecting her each day

In the mirror a thin man shaves
ragged in the cheekbones as a cheap shirt
spilling blood in the grey water
grimacing like a lover reaching his peak

The house was as neat and polished
as a funeral parlour. He heard toast pop
up as she laid out breakfast, her humming
touched him bright as an aneurism

The kitchen fogged in their soap smell
there was sunlight on the trimmed garden.
He fancied she couldn't look at him, all that
busying about, like a fly head-butting a window.

Business End

I imagine her on the 'phone, I conjure her voice a face:
Numbers high for your age, and other confidences

meant to lure me out of the midnight sweats
or the memory of my father on morphine in a hospice.

What expression does she wear, leaning into her lover
(whose readings are normal for his age) for whom

she invokes a different lexicon, her voice intimate,
not phlegmed with static and so damned clinical?

She'll see me undressing in a sterile light; I don
my diaphanous blue gown, lurch like a drunk to a needle

and a table set for one; she'll make rehearsed gestures
all without a blush. This, then, is the business end of love.

Charm Against the Invisible

Now and then the dogs are furious at the invisible
charging the front door to warn away whatever lives in the air
imps of fault and harrowing, plate-eyed ghosts, regrettable

sprites with leaves for hair, grass claws and meaty breath –
the barking drowns them as cold water unwitches them
put in their place, they must, one imagines, go underneath

the garden earth or the concrete driveway; in any case
they prick the ears of dogs in the wee hours
blow cold on my back when I cross the dark space

of hallway to the bathroom. Curdle the milk
even in the fridge. Cause chimney fires at night
that spark star-wards like devil's spit, yellow as yolk –

believing in them is no harm, it keeps you straight
let the dogs do the rest, that's what they're fed for,
lumpen logic only goes so far, the worst of things will wait.

Golden Age

I'd like to call her back, though the corridor is long
and say how sorry I am that I didn't get her name –

Or that I never 'phoned and regret that too
it was not bad manners, it was ugly, as youth often is.

Wretched behaviour on a nightly basis
we called it fun and it was. Now it's an effort to make

a cup of tea; one smokes too much, is prone
to probing medical rituals, there are things to fear.

Does she think so too, as a sixth decade slips in,
or is there, after time, nothing to think about?

What was so raging good about the 'Seventies
or the bed-sits with Joni Mitchell for company?

Was that the glory we now, in our cups, aspire to,
gift-wrapped in a grief for which we have no name?

Lost Pages From a Guide-Book

Over the unsure-of-itself iron balcony
Paris tart-sharp in copper-plate neon,
breakfast is croissants, orange juice and coffee –

The rue-de-Something shivered like a cat
Girls had paced the kerb half the night,
There was a café where *les travestis* held court

You could write a book about it,
The purring sound that rose off the pavement,
Piss and petrol, a street-sweeper mounted

On circular brushes. Somewhere a radioful
Of Maghreb music, manic and loud –
The crack of a window slying over your head

A first day opens like a flower or a tomb
A light anxiety flushed belly-deep –
No postcard this, but an X-ray, a scan to the bone.

Ambush

Like a sniper he squinted through the room's dark
for a clear view of his father's head –
bundled in two fat pillows, an undergrowth of blankets
it was thin, gray and hollowed out
like a deflated football in muddy grass

He couldn't bring himself to turn on a light
startle the imploding man awake –
he felt snug enough when things lost their contours
seeing things more clearly, he'd expose himself
and he was content to be still and watching

Things hissed and ticked, the room was jungle warm
he wanted to smoke but couldn't here
and besides, he might give himself away –
the hospital's tubular chair was no perch to be patient in,
just to think made it creak like a twig snapping

The old man was shallow dips and hills
over this bony topography red lights clicked
and twitched; circling aircraft, homing in –
the man-map moved, shook; the head, an oracle
now, opened lips of dirty wet plaster

The divination was not subtle, though the one-liner
did not shake the world, the ceiling stayed where it was:
If you go now, you can just make the pub –
the dark parted and he saw himself skulking there
a thief of sorts disarmed, nothing for it but to scarper.

Conflict

for Harry Owen

I want to write a poem of protest
but I'm aware I might upset someone
I might upset you

this is the difficulty; how to protest softly
how to smack the metal without
putting a dent in it

how not to become an enemy of the state
of poetry, which has spies everywhere –
how to infiltrate, remain invisible

to pass through checkpoints and not
have my words confiscated
to have no part of me put at risk

yet to make a sound, a mousey squeak
perhaps, but a sound nonetheless –
a sound I can call my own

yet a note which rings out somewhere
under the rubble, in the drains,
in the bombed air

or does nothing else but simply be –
that's sufficient, to be word enough
in landscapes of silence –

to put that word in a single mouth
a miracle in itself,
a rage in a small thing. But can I do this

and stay unharmed, out of the watch
of prizes, honours, a clammy ambition?
Can I hurl my words and run away?

Blues

One day, love, you'll say what you said just now
and you'll be talking to yourself —
the weather won't change, nor the sun go out; but
everything will be unfamiliar, rooms that much more impassive

photos will dry up in their frames
by the time we're back in our separate beds
every window and door will have closed, locks secured
and, if I know you, you'll sleep as if nothing has happened

that's the way, the unofficial version —
everything whimpers in the dark, even the likes of us:
'phones will forget themselves, hours and eras will go by
we'll tell the truth to no one; how easy it was, when the time came.

Dialogue Before Writing

Settling in the window to watch the world
though it stays distant, over the walls and trees
into the valley of things
down in the belly of the whale a busker sings

what can you see from up here? Not much.
It's guess-work, made-up maps and compass-
points. You know every street, but *here*
you toe the uncharted sea of *there*

pushing out, gradually, into a breast-stroke
stagger like a much older man, afraid
of forgetting what you've learned –
the smell of her, perhaps, a corner turned.

Intaglio

for Gerry Murphy, poet

Nothing could have prepared him for the shock
Of her eyelids still open in the unclosed casket
A sort of cosmic insult in the muted light of a funeral
Parlour: he looked and
Backed out and held his tongue. Still. It was wrong.
A better job ought to have been made of it.

The street curled up to a plinthed statue
Of King Billy, jogged past a black-spiked park into
The Black Mountain; it rained, and the rain spat
Like a bigot on the windscreens. She'd hated the place.
Thought the people tight, funless, unknowable.
Maybe she'd taken a last squint, just to be sure.

He lay so long in the damp ditch of her illness
He became lightless: he mummied his mourning
For months after in a fleece of postage-stamps,
Collated with hysteric care into a savaged album.
I have it still, his notations, values, their quaint variety:
The city shifted and shot itself in the foot over and over

All the while the territory of his spine was annexed
By loutish bone, until he leaned on a stick and dwindled
To a fleshed intaglio of himself: still explaining
As we yapped in stilted code on the 'phone
How a rare misprint could cause a riot, of how
A stamp was worth more when still on its envelope.

The Public Scribes

The public scribes sat at antique school desks in a line
like a fair-ground train outside the Post Office in Algiers

writing personal letters, postcards, official pleas and
arguments for those who queued and could neither read

nor write. In apocalyptic heat they earned each dinar
palmed to them in the greatest respect and in no hurry

plain tongues undumbed in speech made visible
learning the personal, the pettily private sins and pieties

of those who could not decipher a 'bus destination or find
their way through a city that flowed like a burst dam –

until the *muezzin* stamped his full-stop in the air. If you
had seen the faces of the disappointed ones tottering

back into the torrent with their dreams and terrors
clamouring in the skull, still unpenned and consequently

without form, you might have wondered, as I did then,
how well the gears of the world would mesh and turn

without the public scribes, their inks and pens put up
for the sake of prayer; and the silence they left behind

rising out of their school-room roosts with the solemnity
of holy men or magi, all sleight-of-hand and dumb contempt.

Truck

Parents cackled in the living-room
while he tried to have me upstairs on his bed
with the promise of a Corgi truck;
call it teenage experimenting if you will
I didn't fancy it, his bribed-up fingery fuck

Over breakfast, between marmalade toast
and scalding porridge, I sniffled out the story;
not a word, a silence soft as a hammer
whatever my father did, and he did something
we never touched that house again in any weather

I kept the truck. It was solid, useful transport
for carrying small soldiers and farm animals –
it never recalled that prick's tell-no-one lust
it was innocent of all that, it was its mere self
die-cast, to scale, a thing you could trust.

What Good

We don't talk about it now
but love was like that, then
between the scabrous desk and steel-nibbed pen
we drew a small thing in the air
though we couldn't quite read the scribble there
it was a form of magic anyhow.

The age of in-between and
neither here nor there, it was
the adolescent heart's banter, indefinite article, pause
he carried my bag, I hefted his books
down a long street angeled by crows and rooks
over a red-brick invisible city; we'd land

At a bus-stop with nothing to say –
others felt similar strangeness, had we known –
a right of passage; by term's end we'd outgrown
such ambiguity, got sense, found girls, matured:
might we meet in our new old age, death-assured
united in some waiting-room, loveless as an X-ray ?

In The Grub House

There were often drunks sleeping it off under the subs' benches
hot-metal printers, black ink vapour on the catwalk handrail
over the press, a stone anarchy that worked, typewriters
and girls in headphones, nicknames, real spikes,
windows on the river, hieroglyphs of 12pt Blk u/l set left
a drudge of subbing Racing Results on Saturday afternoons
(never a shift up-table where the hot news was tapped out)
sports subs, news subs, galley-proofs, case-room blues
shirt-and-tie, 'phones thick and black as lumps of coal
by-lines or *By Our Correspondent* –
foreign news stories 'phoned in from a local pub; biros,
pencil-stubs, glue-pots, cigarette butts, House Style books
cracked mugs, stained cups, purloined Cinzano ashtrays –
Victorian urinals down the stairs, stalls
and on the backs of the doors, schoolboy porno scrawls
Herculean pricks uncut, mythically-embosomed, uncensorable wenches.

Inquisition

Whatever you'd kept far is near now –
a haunting of brisk nurses in clean corridors
pretty, efficient, waving brown-backed files
an interview of details at a brown table
brown-headed tea, a biscuit on a sheet-white saucer

days counted like journeys end in a leaning
of men against a wall of pinned notices
a dumb waiting through a miasma of speculation
in a short-walk hallway of closed doors
waiting for a sign, this due process of selection

here, then, the white-sheeted table, a clinkle of metal:
on a small screen a projection of ends or starts
here you're put to the question, the jab and probe
a language way over your head, a tear of blood
on white cloth; nothing to worry about, find your feet.

Now That The War Is Over

'I'm sorry, but the chick just got in the way.'
   – US Marine in Iraq, who shot a woman in a crowd

Now that the war is over, come back to me,
Now there's only the dead to count –
Not ours, but theirs –
We'll be as before, sipping cold drinks on verandahs
Sloppy with sunlight, or in rooms
With soft incense burning in the afternoon,
An evening paper chunks on the mat:
I watch you close your eyes and open your mouth,
As if love were pain, and myself
Moving against you with loving violence
Will descend into a sort of foolishness –
The parked cars will shine under the bright hammers
Of light, the gardens will crop themselves,
A cobweb rain will cover everything by midnight:
Let them riot in colour, while you dream
In black-and-white. We make love in tones
Of yellow-brown and blue –
A gun looks oil-black, waved in a man's face
It blurs and glints like your eyes as we lie
In the after-blast of love, bunkered
In the blown sheets. You will ask for a cigarette
And over your head the peace will fall
Like a picture unsurely nailed to the wall.
The midnight TV news blinks above us
In the slow black of our room, and the rain
Comforts us, hissing, gossipy, on the red roof.

In Sousse

We flip-flopped half a day through Sousse
bought a carpet, a mint-tea-and-haggle affair
the heat was brilliant, the sea chugged
on a long promenade. In smothery back streets
old men played dominoes, clack-snap in the bone-dry air.

We read books on the hotel's beach
a noisy family poked and argued under a fat umbrella
there was nothing to do, which was why we'd come
though now and then we'd toe the green water
or doze in a thin lather of lotion, while the sun burned

Red our sunless skin. Afternoons were siestas
lulled barks of beer-swillers on balconies
now and then the grumpy roar of a tourist bus –
night fell very quickly, a surprise of coolness
we slept on the sheets and kept the windows wide

Who'd go home from such routine indolence
withdraw as if surfacing from a lazy sea
pack up the books, blankets and unfilled postcards
take a heat-wrapped bus to an airport, leave
for the well-mapped dullness of you and me –
who'd abandon such a surfeit of grace so easily?

Riviera Incident

When the old Monégasque fisherman
was hauled in, dead, on his small boat
I learned of it from the doorman
who'd known him, and who for the evening
was tasked with opening ornamented
doors for our gilded mob
and who'd sniffled quietly to himself
as the chapel filled and the orchestra tuned up.

The music ravished and delighted
the applause – some women wore white gloves –
was appropriate and damp with dignity
while he stood at the back under a fresco,
it was not his place to applaud;
soon, again, he turned his duty to the doors
and I said something to him, I cannot recall
what, and went out with the rest into the heat.

The bay was full of yachts, some
tolerated helicopters fat and black as tickbirds
our evening was unending
the sun would not descend
drinks came iced in glasses
thin-stemmed, fragile as tears –
the head of the doorman who mourned
the old fisherman bobbed and sank
like a black olive down the daiquiri-yellow hill.

The Shoe-Maker of Cernaça

He saw the world, such as it was
framed in the yellow stone of a single window
and from this work-perch made deductions
rhythmic as his small hammering –
below him, at a mile's distance, the river
he had never crossed, bleated
and spilled itself like a sacrifice,
but no spell in the world could stop
the tourist 'buses and the cameras: he was
a peculiarity of shadows and skin.

In the dark of the morning he drank milk
and prayed. He was not pious,
there was nothing else to do. Sick and ailing
shoes lay on warped racks. He spoke
to them, asked them questions, and learned
of cruelties they'd endured; little wonder
they broke in the end. He caressed them,
eased them into his care, his leathery surgeries,
and perhaps that is why he had so many.
He himself went barefoot. Out of respect.

So Now, In London

So now, in London, what do you see –
Saucy Eros, rampant Picadilly
Soho, if you have the time
And (not really your thing) an art gallery

It rains, you say, there's a London fog
The hotel's fine, you miss your cuddly dog
You can't have everything
You've left behind grey nights, bad roads, bog

Or me, perhaps, if I'm worth a text
(A medium chill as telephone sex)
London's where it's at now
But where comes next, and next, and next?

Good Weather

Take good weather while you can
let the washing idle on the line
drag a steel chair into the sun-
light
pour coffee, let the dog snuffle the clematis,
calendula, a hairy feral cat thief-sneak
through the whimpering geraniums

punch a door through the white
walls, drag in new light
light reluctant when winter flops down here
with its mean fogs and 'flus
it will need minding –

here we are, then, walled off
from neighbours and creepy wind:
this is good
under the breathing of the little house
there's the noisy energy of children
yellow light
reaches a hand across the glass tabletop

we should do this more often.

Gone Native

Up before dawn, the garden gone Jurassic and ominous
Uncharted, whole tribes could be hiding down there
The smell of weak sun varnishing the larger leaves, sending
Up the old primæval musk, snakes and apples, an oafish Eden –

I'll take a scythe to it one day, one afternoon, gather myself
Slow-stepping into the undergrowth, bible in a free hand
Solar topee hammered on my head, bloated with God's edicts
Listen for vipers and worse things slicking in the sharp grass

The source of the Nile is somewhere between my window
And the breeze-block wall; I might do a Kurtz and disappear
I ought to disappear, I've been mapping myself for too long
Only the thin frugal smoke of my fire, only a rusting blade

Here I'll give myself new names in magical computations
Sit cross-leggéd on the mulch and work through malaria
Chant obscenities to make rain, hear other people's radios
Edge closer, the plunder of distant traffic, the grass growing

There'll be a girl laughing in a spasm over the horizon
A dog's bark, the sound of cutlery on dinner plates –
By then I'll be somewhere and someone else, gone native
Ghosty in my green-black back garden, a man translated.

Some Houses

Some houses you walk past in a hurry
something radioactive about them
inside they're ready to blow
that's why the upstairs windows are always open
dogs scavanging in the garden
a wreckage of pram shards, wooden pallets
oil stains where a car used to be, now hauled away, wounded –

they're ready to blow, or leak, or otherwise pollute
your peace of mind
the curtains are never drawn, the plasma-screen TV
is an eye watching you –
houses on the dazed side of the street
they emit a hum of discontent in a minor key;
some houses you walk past in a hurry.

Blindness Falling

'*Ta peur de n'être pas*
te fait copier les bêtes . . . .'
EUGÈNE GUILLEVIC: *Carnac*

First sight of the desert was no sight at all
white sky like blindness falling, nothing there –

the 'bus roof rattled with the scary scrabble of macaques
that dropped on us from the last of the cliffs

the road was an unravel of black into oblivion
you, my daughter, dozed flush-faced in the oily heat

as the water-bottles were passed from seat to seat
hard bread rolls full of egg and salt, a tobacco reek

then the wine wore off, the heart took it all in
we fell off the world's edge and gathered speed

like all things descending, flailing as if drowning
in this white ocean of the non-existent

those ragged suitcases of the poor jiggering
among the baskets of fruit on the luggage racks

over our heads, the windows clear as water
your blue eyes when you awoke a wonder

to the tattooed woman who covered one eye
who knew this nowhere like the back of her hand.

Conversation

'Regard! mais regard! et respire! ....'
ROBERT DESNOS: *L'Évade*

In front of the café, there is often a mime
and sometimes, when he's elsewhere, a fire-juggler.

The mime is unmoving until a child throws a coin
then he jerks once as if he's been shot.

The juggler takes a long time harnessing
a crowd, teasing them, doing nothing, but loudly.

It's a slow graduation, an evolution, towards the act
of juggling blazing torches three at a time —

the mime may move once in twenty minutes,
he is his own conclusion, like a word stamped on a page.

To stand for so long, not a muscle moving,
he must shift his mind out of the street and elsewhere,

how else could he sustain that unmoving nothing,
an utter absence of collaboration, that refusal?

The fire-juggler is his opposite, all flail and shout
and complicity; one day, if we're lucky, he'll burn.

Taken together, they are a coming in and going out,
a reversal and a forward acceleration; a conversation.

Georgian Door

In a bedroom cocked like a hat over a roofdom of nightclubs
We listened through open windows to muted music, bass beats
The sheets dragged and snagged and wrackled round our feet
We could hear the snapping shouts of emptying invisible pubs

Here I cupped your loved face in fingers moist with you
Explored with my mouth the abandonment of your skin
The air in that room turned tropical with our sour heat
And we fell asleep with new light slying up the slate roof

Then this room emptied itself of each of us and every thing
That made or mapped us, the sound of nothing entered in
I could knock forever on the numberless door without answer
A holy space echoed like a vacant tomb, our names erased

I searched Dublin for a sign, tore up the pavement for our bones
My ear hugged every nook we'd snuggled in, I was dumb for days –
That Georgian door I entered by no longer pulsed with a light
Miraculous to me. We'd kiss, you'd leave, I'd listen to it close.

Room Service

It shouldn't take so much to clean a room
but bedrooms are a unique weight —

feathers from a burst duvet lie light
and elusive everywhere, the carpet

is christmassed with their nervy explosion
and books too, scraggled, cobwebby

canyons cowboyed by tentative spiders
raiding-parties that ride out in the dark —

unused matches and plastic lighters
divide and reproduce themselves where

none could be found before. The white
hillocks of pillows have turned yellow like

pissy snow. The bed wears a sense of
abandonment, dismissal, neglect:

bedsheets grotesque as death-throes,
a scene to flee from, a fleshless carnage

the framed photographs hang at odd
angles, as if skewed in a blast that crazed

the room; or perhaps the whole house has
tilted, clothing has scuttled into a wardrobe

unhung, unhangered, and there are too many
loveless shoes. Something and nothing happened

here, the ceiling has been questioned too long
the windows need opening to let the ghost out

the ashtray needs emptying, the bedside lamp
craves a light-bulb. Maybe the blood needs

mopping up. Perhaps this is a job for a professional.

Green Deep

Now they've come
to trim the garden, cut

around the flaccid plum-trees
and the two gifted oaks

reveal the Coke tins and what
else the barbarians hurled

like grief into our green deep.
The wail of electric saws

under our walls
is teeth-chilling, iron into bark,

a sour whittling, artless
as a machine-gun –

to give us more space, you say
more light and *lebensraum*,

the diktats of a sitting-room
become a policy of clearance.

Bird Incident

Sounded as if someone had pushed in the front door
it was unlocked, not properly closed over, but a bird
harvesting the heft of its flight, had walloped in
saw the skylight, climbed up on a shaft of grey light
which he mistook for a stairway, and now it had
wrapped itself in a shroud of dust-webs and lost the
fragile aerodynamics of muscled bone and knitted feather

making so much noise, like a child railing at the bars
of a cot, like a man gone mad at the squeeze of his cell
or someone buried under rubble, this clamour and rage
turned frightening to look at, so that I was afraid, a giant
wielding a broom-handle, not hitting but helping, until
without guidance but from some blown instinct it saw
the gift of the open door through which it had entered

and scraked by and out, leaving the hallway quiet again
trailing a scarf of dust and web but unencumbered, free.

A Poem For You

Do not tell me my name
Only my tongue is strong enough to carry it

Do not open my door
My heart alone has the key

Do not measure my acre
Only my stride is long enough

Do not look over my wall
Only these eyes can see that far

Do not stare at my children
For only my eyes can see them

Do not plough my fields
For my earth will not yield to you

Do not harm my olive tree
For it is watered by my blood

Do not wound my flesh
For the mark is inscribed on your soul

Do not offer words to humble me
For no language can drown my shout

Do not tell me where I live
For I know every inch of my own flesh

Do not call me invisible
You cannot see the wind when it blows

Do not offer me vinegar for wine
Nothing is as bitter as the taste in my mouth

Do not offer me sand for bread
For I will make bread even from sand

Do not tell me who I am
For I am written in the Book of the World.

*Written for the visit of the Lajee Dabka Dancers to Galway,
from the Aida refugee camp in Palestine.*

Requiem

Out across the bay they'll find him
dribbled like a football by a rogue tide
there are rocks in the river
the size of cars and small vans
not much of what we knew of him left to look at

Then there's the other one, a week
lying in his rot and stink in a small apartment
we all knew his address
but it was always much too far
I'd imagined him successful, in his way –

Once you start on lists, it's uphill work:
but I know that some were dead for years
and we argued with ghosts
all the bar-talk was mere obituary
the bombast and bluster a build-up of gases.

We get it wrong about one another
right up to the end, and beyond the end
we misinterpret, leave gaps where memory blurs
fill in those shaped like myths –
we're embarrassed when there's so little to say.

Born Again

Out the kitchen window there's a red-door shed
As guilty as a killer's play-room
A clutch, if that's the word, of doomed plants in pots
The hint of a pushbike scanned on the wall

If this is the view they've mortgaged, this
With the promise of a dead four-door humped on bricks
Oiling up the no-man's-lane, good luck to them –
It's not what the brochure offered

Pour ritual on top of this, his, hers, ours
And foundations slip
Fungal cracks eat the walls – like subtle lesions, if you like –

There's not a tree in sight, two fat crows on an aerial
A Hitchcock script scrawled on the curtains
If it weren't for a glint of lottery luck . . . .

Give it time and again the sun comes out
Glimmering peevish grass, polishing the brasses
Put the knives back in the drawer, buy a Rolling Stones

T-shirt for a fiver, one with a fat red tongue on it:
There's nothing that can't be plastered over –
But the shed that can't be born again, sepulchre
That it is, its unrollable stone the size of your heart.

My Father Ought To Have Liberated Dachau

My father ought to have liberated Dachau
but he did his bit elsewhere
in shot-asunder Sunderlands, their fat bloody bellies
his to wash out, heroism of a different sort —

My father might have done many things
worthy of a photograph
instead he dodged the monumental and settled
for the ordinary trudge, heroism of a different order —

My father was a well-read man and good at maths
reduced to doing the Pools
or telling his child-son how the *Tirpitz* ended
his war memory monumental, his delight herculean

And when her legs melted into cancer
he didn't send for me
knew better; youth is indifferent, death a myth —
the daily dressings, pain's mess, love and duty.

Early Hours

The brazen orange highway lighting
the cheek of it –
    early hours drift of mist
    off the dead garages, reluctant chimney
    smoke; fag-end of a middling day

the hospital is a cruise-liner dead
in the roads –
    everything is floating, the granite
    cathedral a cliff-face of fuck-you:
    someone skulking home in a hoodie

the nerve of this night I'm driving
through, the insolence –
    at least it's dry, dry as bone
    the sky is made of bone, bone-
    brittle, skanky, could do with a wash.

Sign Language

They'll build housing estates on flood plains
seeping acres waiting to drown

names in Irish signal the wet places
where neither nouse nor grazing is safe
but the planners cannot read them

So again we have buried back-roads, cattle
fidgeting on new islands, compensation claims –

English sniggers from road-signs
leads the Irish astray, the plan-and-bedamned
boys have a tongue of their own.

Calum sGaire

Dublin, 1976

– 'S fhada ò mo luaidh anochd mi –

How that summer witched us
through the denim-blue air of Grafton Street
musical pubs, the dizzy going-nowhere
of day into night
your breath on my breath, a white sheet
tumbled on a high Georgian floor
stone steps, black railings, a Georgian door –

in Enniskerry of the hushing hill
a café window, Powerscourt gardens falling
away in a giggle of water
the urgency of time-tables, a 'bus
to take us back, time was not time enough
yet soon enough the city steepling
and rough-roofed and the browny river –

for what damage were we prepared
silly as infants and full of high mockery
while that island song rowed round my head
day into night
and back again, circling its own calamity –
and still we slept in our sheltering place
breath to breath, face to face.

*'Calum sGaire' is the name of the composer of the song of that name,
in English 'Malcolm Macauley', born in Bernera, near the Isle of
Lewis, in 1822. It's a song of unrequited love and emigration. The
poem is not an interpretation of the song, but was inspired by it.*

FRED JOHNSTON was born in Belfast in 1951. Most recently, his poems have appeared in *The Spectator*, *The New Statesman*, and a short story in *Stand* magazine; some more new work is also due to appear there. In 1972, he received a Hennessy Literary Award for prose. In the mid-Seventies, with Neil Jordan and Peter Sheridan, he co-founded The Irish Writers' Co-operative (Co-Op Books.) In 2002, he was a co-recipient of the Prix de l'Ambassade, Ireland. His most recent collection of short stories, *Dancing In The Asylum*, was published by Parthian a couple of years ago, and his most recent collection of poetry is *Alligator Days* (Revival Press). In 1986, he founded Galway's annual literature festival, Cúirt; in 2002, he was writer-in-residence to the Princess Grace Irish Library at Monaco. Fred has published nine collections of poems, four novels and two collections of short stories, one of which has been translated into French. He has also composed poetry in French and published it in France in magazines such as *Ouste*, *Hopala!*, *Le Moulin de Poésie* and *Le Grognard*, among others.

www.**salmon**poetry.com

*"Like the sea-run Steelhead salmon that thrashes upstream to its spawning
ground, then instead of dying, returns to the sea – Salmon Poetry Press
brings precious cargo to both Ireland and America in the poetry it publishes,
then carries that select work to its readership against incalculable odds."*

Tess Gallagher